SAMSON AND DELILAH

Read-Along Storybook - Sing-Along Songs - PC Fun!

Published by

PC Multimedia Entertainment
TREASURES, INC.

1795 N. Lapeer Road, Oxford, Michigan 48371 USA

Samson and Delilah
Story adapted by Darcy Weinbeck
Audio CD Reading Performed by David DuChene
Songs Produced and Performed by Deron (D.B.) Harris
Vocal Performances by Melissa Cusick and Deron (D.B.) Harris

ISBN 978-1600720949

First Published 2008

Long ago there was a man named Manoah who lived with his wife in Israel. They both wanted to have a child but were unable. They were good people who worked hard and worshiped God. God knew this and wanted to help them.

TURN PAGE

1

One day, an angel came to Manoah's wife and told her that she would be blessed with a son. "Eat only healthy food while you wait for your son," the angel said, "and when the boy is born, if you feed him healthy foods and never cut his hair, he will have great strength."

Manoah's wife was excited by the angel's message and went to tell her husband the good news. Manoah didn't believe her, so God decided to send a second angel to talk to both of them. After hearing from the second angel, Manoah also believed.

TURN PAGE

Manoah and his wife followed the angel's instructions very carefully. They knew that if they did as the angels had said, their son would have the strength of the Lord running through him.

In time, the baby boy was born and they named him Samson. They fed him only healthy food and they never cut his hair. As Samson grew older, his hair grew longer, and his strength became greater, just as the angel had said it would.

Years passed and many of Samson's fellow Israelites were captured and enslaved by the wicked people known as Philistines. This troubled Samson, and when he was old enough, he left home with the hope of using his great strength to free his people.

Samson had been gone for many days and was on his way home when he came across a group of Philistines by the side of the road. He was going to order them to free his people, but before he could, he was distracted by a beautiful young Philistine woman.

Samson approached the young woman and introduced himself. After a short conversation he found that he liked this woman very much. He told her that he was traveling home to look after his parents, but would like to visit with her again. The woman happily gave him directions to her house. Samson bade her farewell and promised he would visit her soon.

Samson returned to his parents and told them about the beautiful Philistine woman he had met. Manoah said, "Samson, are you so confused by beauty that you would submit to this Philistine woman's charms? Go back to her and learn that things aren't always as they seem."

Samson soon set off once more. He was excited to see the beautiful young woman again. At the same time, God was pleased to know that the mighty Israelite would soon be amidst the evil Philistines.

On the way to the woman's house, Samson noticed a large, fierce lion walking on the road. When the lion spotted Samson, it turned and attacked him. Samson felt no fear, for the strength of God was within him. He fought the lion with his bare hands and easily defeated it. **TURN PAGE**

After his victory against the lion, Samson set the beast on the ground. He watched with surprise as the lion changed into a beehive overflowing with honey. As he filled a nearby jar with honey for nourishment on his long trip, he realized that even a dangerous lion can be turned to sweetness if such is God's will.

Samson continued on and soon arrived at the beautiful Philistine woman's house. She greeted him warmly and Samson was very happy to be with her again. But Samson didn't know that the woman had an evil plan to turn him over to the Philistines.

TURN PAGE

The woman offered Samson dinner. As he was eating, thirty
Philistine men burst into the woman's home and attacked him.
Samson easily defeated the Philistines and learned a valuable
lesson as well. As a lion can be filled with sweetness, a beautiful
person can be filled with evil.

Twenty years passed and Samson's legend grew as he fought and won many battles against the enemies of the Israelites. In time, Samson met a woman named Delilah and fell in love. Though it was hard for him to forget the betrayal of the last Philistine woman, Delilah was good to him and Samson trusted her.

When the Philistines learned of Samson's love for Delilah, they thought of a plan to finally defeat this powerful enemy. They went to see Delilah and offered her a thousand coins if she would reveal to them the source of Samson's great strength. Thinking only of the money, Delilah accepted the offer.

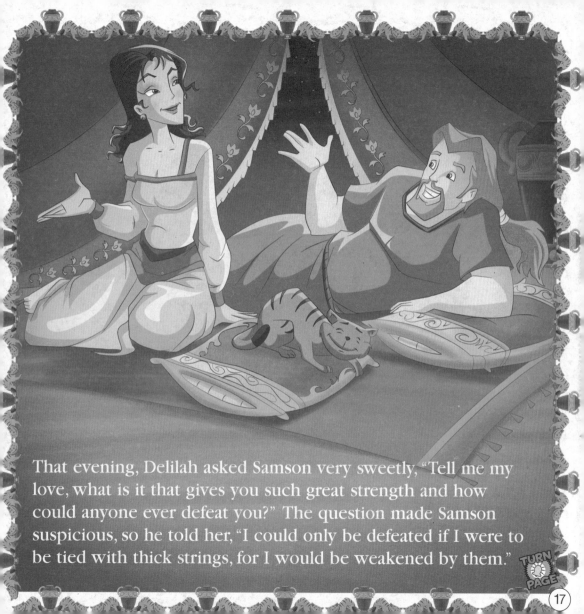

That evening, Delilah asked Samson very sweetly, "Tell me my love, what is it that gives you such great strength and how could anyone ever defeat you?" The question made Samson suspicious, so he told her, "I could only be defeated if I were to be tied with thick strings, for I would be weakened by them."

That night, while he was sleeping, Delilah tied Samson up
with thick strings as several Philistines hid nearby. When he
was wrapped tightly, Delilah shouted, "Samson, help me!
The Philistines are here!" Samson sat up and broke the
strings with ease.

Delilah was upset that Samson had lied to her, and the next day she scolded him, "Samson, you have made a fool of me! Tell me the truth about the secret of your power." Samson would not give away his secret, so he told her, "Tie me up with strong, new rope and I will lose all strength, for it will weaken me."

TURN PAGE

That night, as Samson slept, Delilah tied him snugly with strong
new rope while the Philistines hid just as the night before.
Delilah shouted, "Samson, the Philistines are upon you!" Samson
sat up and freed himself as if the rope were no more than thread.

The next day Delilah again scolded Samson, "You say that you love me, but you don't even trust me. Tell me the source of your great strength or else I will leave you!" Samson was heartbroken. Though he knew it was not wise, he finally told Delilah the truth. "Cut my hair," he said sadly, "and I will lose God's strength."

That evening as Samson slept, Delilah again tied Samson with strong rope and had a servant cut Samson's hair. As his long hair fell to the floor, God's great strength fell with it.

Delilah shouted, "Samson, the Philistines are here!" Samson sat up but, try as he might, he couldn't break free from the rope.

The Philistines that were hiding nearby captured Samson and made him a slave. Every day Samson worked beside the other Israelite slaves grinding wheat for the Philistines' bread. Though his body was weak Samson never lost his greatest strength, the strength of his faith in God.

TURN PAGE

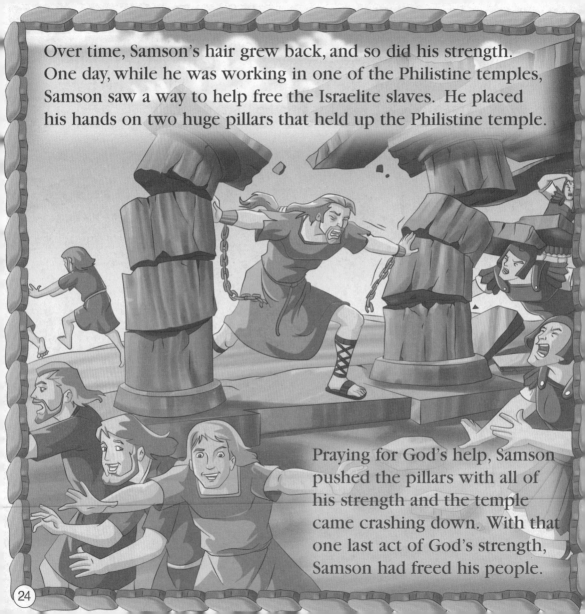

Over time, Samson's hair grew back, and so did his strength. One day, while he was working in one of the Philistine temples, Samson saw a way to help free the Israelite slaves. He placed his hands on two huge pillars that held up the Philistine temple.

Praying for God's help, Samson pushed the pillars with all of his strength and the temple came crashing down. With that one last act of God's strength, Samson had freed his people.